figures

of the

true

Devotional Thoughts
Inspired by Nature

AMY CARMICHAEL

PUBLICATIONS

Figures of the True: Devotional Thoughts Inspired by Nature
Published by CLC Publications

U.S.A.
P.O. Box 1449, Fort Washington, PA 19034

UNITED KINGDOM
CLC International (UK)
Unit 5, Glendale Avenue, Sandycroft, Flintshire, CH5 2QP

Printed in the United States of America

ISBN (paperback): 978-1-936143-82-5
ISBN (e-book): 978-1-61958-136-4

Unless otherwise noted, Scripture quotations are from the
Holy Bible, King James Version, 1611.

Scripture quotations marked BCP are from
The Book of Common Prayer, Church of England, 1662.

Italicized words in Scripture quotes are the emphasis of the author.

Editor's Foreword

A my Carmichael's call to missions—first in Ireland among the mill workers, then briefly in Japan, and finally in India where she rescued children from forced temple service and prostitution—allowed this humble servant to see beauty in brokenness and to see hope in the darkest of situations.

Birthed out of Amy's desire to share the lessons she gleaned from photographs sent to her by her friend Dr. Hans aus der Fünte, *Figures of the True: Devotional Thoughts Inspired by Nature* is a blend of text and imagery—a "multimedia presentation" that existed before the terminology to explain it.

After unearthing the original negatives in an old filing cabinet in our editorial department, we had them professionally redeveloped to give our readers a better picture of the artwork that inspired Amy's writings. While the antique photographs lack the sharpness of modern technology, we felt it important to preserve the authentic pieces Amy found so compelling.

In this new edition, we're pleased to include a few of Amy's poems that reveal her heart for redemption and her yearning to grow ever closer to Christ, as well as her ability to perceive God's promises through His natural creations.

Our graphic designer followed Amy's example of seeing art in nature by photographing a tree growing along the road to our headquarters for the cover image. Moving from black and white (signifying difficulty and death) to color (new life), the cover reveals that in spite of difficult circumstances, Christians—plugged into the True Vine (John 15:1)—are never without hope.

We release this booklet in its new format in the expectation that these *Figures of the True* would point heavenward to the Lord of ultimate beauty. "For Christ is not entered into the holy places made with hands, which are the figures of the true; but into heaven itself, now to appear in the presence of God for us" (Heb. 9:24, kjv).

Laura Pollard
Associate Editor, CLC Publications

Preface

"I send these photographs in the hope that they may be a pleasure," it was so Dr. Hans aus der Fünte wrote, as he sent in his kindness a packet of photographs. And the one to whom he sent them wanted to give them that very hour to every one who is in any sort of trouble, and who has eyes to see and a heart to understand, and who knows Him who ponders the voice of our humble desires.

For surely they are not only lovely pictures of fragments of a lovely creation, they are patterns of things we all know if we have ever really lived: they are Figures of the True.

Perhaps, for one never knows where a book may wander, this little book may discover one who does not know his Comfort. It is written, "The Lord turned and looked upon Peter" (Luke 22:61). The Lord turns and looks upon you. There is no hardness in that look, there is no hardness in the words that have led myriads into peace, "*Come unto me, all ye that labour and are heavy laden, and I will give you rest*" (Matt. 11:28).

There is no other way of rest. All other ways break down. But why seek another way? Fear not, whatever your extremity be; He will not let the water-flood overflow you, neither will He let the deep swallow you up, nor the pit shut her mouth upon you. He shall deliver the needy when he crieth, the poor also and him that bath no helper.

And if the very word "come" be perplexing, let old, old words explain it:

> Believe and thou comest; love and thou art drawn. Think it not a rough and uneasy violence: it is sweet, alluring; the sweetness draws thee. Is not a hungry sheep drawn, when the grass is shewn it? It is not, I ween, driven on in body, but is bound tight by longing. So do thou too come to Christ. Do not conceive of long journeyings. When thou believest, then thou comest. For to Him who is everywhere, men come by loving, not by travelling.[1]

Is not this a good word for one who cannot "travel" far?

A. C.
Dohnavur Fellowship,
Dohnavur, Tinnevelly District, S. India

---

1. St. Augustine (354–430), sermon 131.

Things Not Seen

Great Son of Man who walked our dust,
   Thy love will not forget
The power the temporal has to thrust,
   And overset.

O let Thy touch make things we see
   Transparent to our eyes,
That secrets of Eternity
   We may surprise.

And let the things which are not seen
   Shine like the stars at night,
Till all the space that lies between
   Be filled with light.

1

You were like a leafy bush, and many little things came to you for shelter. You were not great or important, but you could help those little things. And it was the joy of your life to help them.

Now you cannot do anything at all. Some desolation, illness, poverty or something that you cannot talk about has overwhelmed you, and all your green leaves have gone. So you cannot shelter even the least little bird; you are like this bush with its bare twigs, no use to anyone—that is what you think.

But look again at this bare bush. Look at the delicate tracery of lines on the snow. The sun is shining behind the bush, and so every little twig is helping to make something that is very beautiful. Perhaps other eyes that you do not see are looking on it too, wondering at what can be made of sun and snow and poor bare twigs. And the spring will come again, for after winter there is always spring.

When will the spring come? When will your bush be green with leaves again? When will the little birds you love come back to you? I do not know.

Only I know that sun and snow are working together for good, and the day will come when the very memory of helplessness to help and bareness and poverty and loneliness will pass as a dream of the night, and all that seemed lost will be restored.

Now, in the multitude of the sorrows that you have in your heart, let these comforts refresh your soul. They will not fail you for He will not fail you who is the God of the sun and of the snow.

Winter

When my leaves fall, wilt Thou encompass them?
   The gold of autumn flown, the bare branch brown,
The brittle twig and stem,
 · The tired leaves dropping down—
Wilt Thou encompass that which men call dead?
   I see the rain, the coldly smoth'ring snow;
My leaves, dispirited,
   Lie very low.

So the heart questioneth, white winter near;
   Till, jocund as the glorious voice of spring,
Cometh His "Do not fear,
   But sing; rejoice and sing,
For sheltered by the coverlet of snow
   Are secrets of delight, and there shall be
Uprising that shall show
   All that through winter I prepared for thee."

2

I was a tall young tree. And many a forest creature as well as many a bird found succor in my strength and comfort under my leaves, for they made a wide, cool shadow, like the shadow of a great rock in a weary land.

But now it is not so. It seems as if it could never be so any more. Frost-bound I stand. I can endure, for I have asked for fortitude, and I trust that I have not asked in vain. But I cannot do what once I did. The trees of the Lord are full of sap; in those gallant trees the birds build their nests. My sap is frozen within me and no bird builds her nest in my cold boughs—those happy birds that sang among my branches, where are they now? O that I had done more for them when power to do was mine!

And I am not alone in this cold solitude, I am only one of many. Those others, frozen as I am, stand as I stand today. Our green days are past; our purposes are broken off, even the thoughts of our hearts.

O give me the comfort of Thy help again, my God, and bring my soul out of prison that I may praise Thy name. There is forgiveness with Thee; unto Thee, O Lord, do I lift up my soul. Hear my voice according to Thy lovingkindness: quicken me, O Lord, according to Thy lovingkindness. Look Thou unto me, and be merciful unto me, as Thou usest to do unto those that love Thy name. The words of men cannot help me now; miserable comforters are they all. Speak Thou to me, O God, for with Thee is the fountain of life. Let Thy tender mercies come unto me that I may live. O God, be not far from me. O my Strength, haste Thee to help me."[1]

* * *

"My son, thou hast made thy prayer unto Me in an acceptable time. In the multitude of My mercy I have heard thee; in the truth of My salvation I have delivered thee. O cast thy burden upon the Lord, and He shall sustain thee. It is He that hath made summer *and winter*."[2]

* * *

"Summer *and winter*? Then Thou hast not shut me up into the hand of the enemy. I had thought that I and those others were so shut up in this prison of frost that we could not come forth."

"But My frost-bound ones are the bondmen of their Lord. (One of My bondmen said, 'I am an ambassador in bonds.') My mercy compasseth them about. Every part of thy being is embraced in the shining of My mercy. Thou

---

1. Quoted from: Ps. 142:7; 130:4; 86:4; 119:149; 119:132; 36:9; 119:77; 71:12
2. Quoted from: Ps. 69:13; 55:22

hast said in thine heart, 'All these things are against me,' but one day thou shalt say, 'Blessed be morsels of ice; hail, snow and vapors.' Thou shalt know that all these things were fulfilling My word."

"I know it now. From Thee came the ice and the hoary frost of heaven. My life was as the face of the deep when it is frozen, but Thou hast given me grace to help in time of need. I will trust and not be afraid. Blessed be God who hath not turned away my prayer nor His mercy from me. The day is Thine; the night also is Thine. Thou hast prepared the light and the sun. Thou hast set all the borders of the earth; Thou hast made summer *and winter*. My times are in Thy hand. Thy word hath quickened me."

For a little while he was silent to his God, and then he said, "I will fear no evil, for Thou art with me" (Ps. 23:4).

And his God answered him in words whose depths no man has sounded, "*I will never leave thee, nor forsake thee*" (Heb. 13:5).

And then, "to long-loved music set," a song began to sing within him. He could hear every word distinctly; "My soul He doth restore again" was one line of that song. And it ended peacefully,

> Goodness and mercy all my life
>   Shall surely follow me:
> And in God's house for evermore
>   My dwelling-place shall be.[3]

---

3. Francis Rous, "The Lord's My Shepherd, I'll Not Want" (1650)

The Mist Will Pass

Where are ye, O ye mountains? Not a peak
Has looked on me throughout this heavy day.
Where is your purple? I see nought but grey;
The place you once made glad is cold and bleak.

See, wind and sun perform their ministry.
Watch the tossed mist shape silver frames of cloud,
Until the crags, like friendly faces, crowd
To look through clear, large windowpanes at Thee.

• • • •

The sun streams out and shines through wetted leaves,
And strikes the fern like golden rust aslant.
Hark to the birds; the wood is jubilant,
As if the world held nowhere one that grieves.

Then, O my heart, be comforted; be strong.
The mist will pass; the mountains will remain;
The sun will shine; the birds will sing again.
In mist, in rain, look up and sing thy song.

3

*T*here was one who was not afraid of any evil tidings, for her heart stood fast believing in the Lord. And her trust was in the tender mercy of God for ever and ever.

Often He had arisen as light in the darkness.

Often she had called upon Him in troubles, and He had delivered her and heard her what time the storm fell upon her.

He had been merciful, loving and righteous, and she had said, "Who is like unto the LORD our God, that hath His dwelling so high; and yet humbleth Himself to behold the things that are in heaven and earth?"(Ps. 113:5, BCP). And now she found herself standing alone, looking into a great mist.

Fold after fold the hills lay there before her, but always in mist. She could see no path, except a little track in the valley below. She thought that she was quite alone, and for a while she stood looking, listening and feeling this loneliness and uncertainty harder to bear than any acute distress had ever been.

Then, softly, voices began to speak within her, now discouraging, now encouraging.

"My flesh and my heart faileth: but God is the strength of my heart, and my portion for ever" (Ps. 73:26).

"My lovers and my friends stand aloof from my [soul]: and my kinsmen stand afar off" (38:11).

"Nevertheless I am continually with thee: thou hast holden me by my right hand" (73:23).

"My tears have been my meat day and night, while they continually say unto me, Where is thy God?" (42:3).

"Thou shalt answer for me, O Lord my God" (38:15, BCP).

"Why art thou cast down, O my soul? and why art thou disquieted within me? hope thou in God: for I shall yet praise him who is the health of my countenance, and my God" (42:11).

"My way is hid from [my God]" (Isa. 40:27).

"All my ways are before thee" (Ps. 119:168).

"As for God, his way is perfect . . . and he maketh my way perfect" (2 Sam. 22:31, 33).

"They thirsted not when he led them through the deserts" (Isa. 48:1).

Will they faint when He leads them through the hills?

Then she looked again at the mist, and it was lightening, and she knew that she was not alone, for her God was her refuge and strength, a very present help in trouble. He was about her path; He would make good His lovingkindness toward her, and His lovingkindness was comfortable. Nor could she fear any more, for those dim folds in the hills were open ways to Him. He would not let her be disappointed of her hope.

So it was enough for her to see only the next few steps, because He would go before her and make His footsteps a way to walk in. And of this she was also sure: *He whom she followed saw through the mist to the end of the way.* She would never be put to confusion.

And in that hour a song was given to her. She sang it as she walked: "O what great troubles and adversities hast Thou shewed me, and yet didst thou turn and refresh me: yea, and broughtest me up from the deep of the earth again" (Ps. 71:18, BCP). "The Lord is my strength and my shield; my heart hath trusted in him, and I am helped: therefore my heart danceth for joy, and in my song will I praise Him" (28:7, BCP). "Thou drewest near in the day that I called upon thee: thou saidst, Fear not. O LORD, thou hast pleaded the causes of my soul; thou hast redeemed my life" (Lam. 3:57–58). "O let my mouth be filled with thy praise: that I may sing of thy glory and honour all the day long [*for Thou, Lord, hast never failed them that seek thee*]" (Ps. 71:8, BCP).

And as she walked thus and sang, others whom she did not see because of the mist that still lay on her way heard her singing and were comforted and helped to follow on, even unto the end.

Guided on the Heights

Make me to be Thy happy mountaineer,
    O God most high;
My climbing soul would welcome the austere:
    Lord, crucify
On rock or scree, ice-cliff or field of snow,
The softness that would sink to things below.

Thou art my Guide. Where Thy sure feet have trod
    Shall mine be set—
Thy lightest word my law of life. O God,
    Lest I forget,
And slip and fall, teach me to do Thy will—
Thy mountaineer upon Thy holy hill.

4

A voice said, "*Climb.*"

And he said, "How shall I climb? The mountains are so steep that I cannot climb."

The voice said, "*Climb or die.*"

He said, "But how? I see no way up those steep ascents. This that is asked of me is too hard for me."

The voice said, "Climb or perish, soul and body of thee, mind and spirit of thee. There is no second choice for any son of man. *Climb or die.*"

Then he remembered that he had read in the books of the bravest climbers on the hills of earth, that sometimes they were aware of the presence of a companion on the mountains who was not one of the earthly party of climbers. How much more certain was the presence of his Guide as he climbed the high places of the spirit.

And he remembered a word in the book of mountaineers that heartened him, "My soul is continually in my hand"—it heartened him, for it told him that he was created to walk in precarious places, not on the easy levels of life.

This decision that had to be made, this stern task that would test the fibre of character, this duty that must be performed, this blame that must be accepted without self-defence or resentment—these things were part of the day's work for the true mountaineer. And he said to his foe, love-of-fleshly-ease, "'Rejoice not against me, O mine enemy: when I fall, I shall arise; when I sit in darkness, the LORD shall be a light unto me' (Mic. 7:8). 'I will go in the strength of the Lord GOD' (Ps. 71:16)." And other words came and put new life into him: "'When I said, my foot slippeth; Thy mercy, O LORD, held me up' (Ps. 94:18). 'He maketh my feet like hinds' feet; and setteth me upon my high places' (Ps. 18:33). 'Thou hast enlarged my steps under me, that my feet did not slip' (18:36). 'For thou hast girded me with strength' (18:39). 'Hold thou me up and I shall be safe' (Ps. 119:117)."

And he said, "*I will climb.*"

Darkened Glass

As a young child—who looks from mountain land
  In early dawn
On kindling sky, and sea whose silver band
  Curves as if drawn
By shining fingers round the world—is fain,
Though dazzled, still to gaze and gaze again;

So do Thine older children, Lord, forget
  That naked eyes
May hardly bear the Great Glory set
  In other skies;
And finite, pressing on the infinite,
Know but the wounding of excess of light.

Then, as the child's companion gives a glass
  Darkened to him,
And he, unhurt, sees shapes of wonder pass
  The ocean's rim—
Curled flames afloat in sky of daffodil,
Colors of joy, before invisible—

So, dear Companion of our mountain climb,
  So doest Thou.
Life's darkened glasses we have many a time
  Miscalled, but now
It is not so. Oh, pass before us, pass,
Till we are where they need no darkened glass.

5

I would rejoice in mountains to climb, but I see no mountains. I see only a dreary waste of water, a drearier strip of shore—nothing invigorating, nothing inspiring, nothing hard enough to inspire.

"My life is just like that—not so much hard as dull, and I would have chosen the hard to the last, not mere negation, but achievement at whatever cost. It is the inability to do that is so devastating."

"*Hast thou looked up?*"

"Up? I see a mass of clouds. That is all."

"And nothing beyond the clouds? O look again. Is there no hint of light beyond? Are not the very clouds a marvel of controlled power, pillars of cloud and of fire?"

"My sight faileth me for waiting so long upon my God."

"So long? Ye have need of patience, that, after ye have done the will of God, ye might receive the promise."

"It is written, 'As for me, when I am poor and in heaviness: thy help, O God, shall lift me up (69:30, bcp).' I wait to be lifted up."

"But it is also written, 'As for me, I will patiently abide alway: and will praise thee more and more (71:12, BCP).' *Hast thou tried the lifting power of praise?*"

"My sight faileth for very trouble. How can I praise when I cannot see?"

"We can sing when we cannot see, even a little bird will sing in the grey dusk before the dawn breaks."

"My soul melteth away for very heaviness (119:28, BCP), who can sing when his soul melteth?"

"Tell me, is not thy heart's desire to bring many sons unto glory?"

"That is all my desire, although He make it not to grow."

"Then there is only one way for thee; I know of no other way. If thou wouldest be inwardly victorious and help others to be victors, thou must refuse to be dominated by the seen, and the felt. *Thou must look steadfastly through the visible till the invisible opens to thee.* This is harder than to climb a mountain. It is indeed to climb out of the lowest abyss where the craven soul can crawl, and to walk on the sunlit uplands. It is to live in the spirit of the words of one who was to look out upon a duller stretch of water and a darker strip of shore than thou dost now. Ponder then his words: '*For our light affliction, which is but for a moment, worketh for us a far more exceeding and eternal weight of glory; while we look not at the things which are seen, but at the things which are not seen: for the things which are seen are temporal; but the things which are not seen are eternal*' (2 Cor. 4:17–18).

"Live by the grace of thy Lord in the spirit of these words, for in them is the quality of eternity. Say of the will of thy God, 'I am content to do it.' Go through that depressing dimness without yielding to depression and without depressing others. All the resources of heaven are at thy command to enable thee to do this. Take a single promise of thy God; lean thy full weight upon it, and soon, very soon, thou wilt sing of the Lord because He hath dealt so lovingly with thee."

Show Me the Shining of Thy Face

As when on the mountain, wood and stream,
    A chilly mist doth sudden fall,
And passeth as a shining dream
    The glory that did lighten all,

So is it, Savior, when a chill
    As if of mist oppresseth me;
Where is the garden, where the hill,
    Gethsemane and Calvary?

My joyous colors faint and fade
    In cloudiness of dim distress;
And whispering doubts assail; afraid,
    I walk as in a wilderness.

In such an hour, send forth Thy wind
    That it may purge my heavy air;
The base affections of my mind—
    Let them be sought out, dealt with there.

O sweetness, move in me, renew;
    Look down from heaven, Thy dwelling place;
And do as Thou art wont to do.
    Show me the shining of Thy face.

6

Snowy slopes; a few brave pines trying to go as high as they can; a great curtain of sky so closely drawn—except quite low down where it is raised a little—that it seems to be covering something; a peak that shines out white and clear and triumphant—of what is this the figure, O Lord, my God?

Is it that which surely shall be, the coming of the conquering light? Is that peak the last step up from what we call time, to what we call eternity, with its vision, liberty, revelation, powers and great delights? All that the words mean: "We shall be like him for we shall see him as he is" (1 John 3:2). "And his servants shall serve him: and they shall see his face; and his name shall be in their foreheads" (Rev. 22:3–4)—is that foreshadowed there?

Beyond that curtain does the first of those many mansions stand, which the wise tell us are not simply fixed abodes in some spiritual city, but rather stations along the highways of some vast realm, the country of our Father?

Is this, the unimaginable (for it passes the furthest frontiers of our thought), part of the true that is shown in a figure by this pure peak?

Then, O my heart, welcome all that is sent to prepare and to brace thee for so generous a Tomorrow. Welcome bareness, snow and frost, limitations, frustrations, the strain of uncertainty, steep ways, dull days (but look up on such days, to that which is higher than earth). Welcome these things as the purposed preparation for something made ready for thee before the foundations of the world.

And if the mysteries of the unexplained close round thee in the evening, or, far more truly, as the dawn draws near when thou shalt "waken in His splendor beyond the hurt of night"; if thy mind pushes ahead of thy body and thy longing to do for thy beloved crushes thee and the love that is in thee shatters thee for it seems too mighty, too expanding to be contained in the vessel of the human soul so that love itself is turned to sheer passion of pain—even so, set thy will to welcome all. Let thyself be broken. Let thyself be rent. Lay those keen yearnings in the hands that were wounded for thee. Let another gird thee and carry thee whither thou wouldst not. The hour hasteneth when it will be said, 'And the angels carried him far above the peak, beyond the curtain, to that which is eternal in the heavens.' For it is soon cut off —that silken thread that holds us down, and we fly away. The Lord looses the fettered ones,[1] and sets them free to serve.

And if, as I know well is true, thou wouldst die a hundred deaths if only the nations might be delivered out of their heavy oppressions, and all cruel handling of our fellow creatures who cannot complain but must endure

---

1. Psalm 146: 7, Septuagint

could by one stroke be ended, then stay thyself upon the Word that once spoken can never be annulled: "*Thou, Lord, shalt save both man and beast*" (Ps. 36:7, BCP)—"My covenant will I not break, nor alter the thing that is gone out of my lips: I have sworn once by my holiness, that I will not fail David" (89:34, BCP). "The Lord sitteth above the water-flood; and the Lord remaineth a King for ever. The Lord shall give strength unto his people: the Lord shall give his people the blessing of peace" (29:9–10, BCP).

Is not this strong consolation? Be consoled, therefore. In the end the Creator of the earth will justify His creation of a world, which He foreknew would sin and suffer from generation to generation—else were a demon, not a God, upon the throne. Fear not to dare to think such thoughts. There was one who drank of the cup that is filled to the brim with anguish, and he said, and was not rebuked for saying, "Will the Lord cast off for ever? and will he be favorable no more? Is his mercy clean gone for ever? doth his promise fail for evermore? hath God forgotten to be gracious? hath he in anger shut up his tender mercies?" (77:7–9) But he did not tarry in that place of terrific questions: "And I said, This is my infirmity; but I will remember the years of the right hand of the most High" (77:10). "The Lord is King, be the people never so impatient: he sitteth between the cherubims, be the earth never so unquiet" (99:1, BCP).

Let the winds blow, let the waves thunder, they cannot uproot the rock. The wickedness of the wicked must come to an end, or God would not be God. If they did not consume away like a snail, "So that a man shall say,

Verily there is a reward for the righteous: doubtless, there is a God that judgeth the earth" (Ps. 58:10, BCP), there would be no God for man to worship.

But God IS. The coming of the Lord is as certain as the morning. The night will never return, with its brooding shadows of cruelty and wrong. Light, not darkness, is the ultimate Conqueror. Not always shall our hearts cry out, "*Lord, how long wilt thou look upon this?*" (Ps. 35:17, BCP) for sorrow and sighing shall flee away and the travail of the ages shall cease.

"Cast not away, therefore, your confidence, which hath great recompense of reward" (Heb. 10:35); He must reign. Great voices shall yet declare, "Out of Sion hath God appeared in perfect beauty." And He shall be as the light of the morning, when the sun riseth, even a morning without clouds (2 Sam. 23:4), and the glorious majesty of the Lord shall endure forever.

This assurance is among the things that cannot be shaken—so also is the peace that passeth all understanding, the peace of which He who is the light and thy salvation spoke long ago: "*Peace I leave with you, my peace I give unto you: not as the world giveth, give I unto you. Let not your heart be troubled, neither let it be afraid*" (John 14:27).

Amy Carmichael &
The Dohnavur Fellowship

The work in Dohnavur still continues, but now the Fellowship members are all of Indian nationality. They do not belong officially to any of the organized churches; but in fellowship with others of God's children, they seek to make His love and salvation known to all whom they can reach.

The dedication of girls to the temples is now illegal, but the Fellowship provides a home for children who might otherwise fall into the hands of people who would exploit them in some way.

Girls of all ages from babies to teenagers form a large part of the family in Dohnavur. The need to care for them continues until they are securely launched elsewhere or else have become fellow workers. The aim is still to bring them up to know and love our Lord Jesus and to follow His example as those who desire not to be served but to serve others.

The hospital treats patients from the surrounding countryside. They are from varied religious backgrounds—Hindu, Muslim, Christian. They include rich and poor, highly educated and illiterate. Through this medical work God continues to bring to us the people we long to reach, those whose need is for spiritual as well as physical healing.

Boys are no longer admitted, but the buildings they occupied are now put to full use. In 1981 the Fellowship in partnership with other Christians formed the Santhosha Educational Society to administer a coeducational English-medium boarding school, primarily for the benefit of the children of missionaries of Indian nationality. The buildings provide facilities for over 600 children now studying there. Their parents come from Indian missions and organizations working in many parts of India, including tribal areas.

In matters of finance, we follow the pattern shown from the beginning of the work. Amy Carmichael rejoiced in her Heavenly Father's faithfulness in supplying each need. We praise Him that His faithfulness is the same today.

The Dohnavur Fellowship
Tirunelveli District
Tamil Nadu 627 102
India

The Dohnavur Fellowship
80 Windmill Road
Brentford, Middlesex
TW8 0QH
England

http://www.dohnavurfellowship.org